This book belongs to

....

To John, Joseph and Jacqueline

Published in Australia by Heart-Centred Books
Email: hello@drolivialeeong.com
Website: www.drolivialeeong.com

First published in Australia in 2022
Copyright © Olivia Ong 2022

All rights reserved. No part of this publication may be reproduced, stored in a retrieval system, or transmitted, in any form or by any means without the prior written permission of the publisher, nor be otherwise circulated in any form of binding or cover other than that in which it is published and without a similar condition being imposed on the subsequent purchaser.

National Library of Australia Cataloguing-in-Publication entry

 A catalogue record for this book is available from the National Library of Australia

ISBN: 978-0-6452588-6-8 (paperback)
ISBN: 978-0-6452588-5-1 (hardback)
ISBN: 978-0-6452588-7-5 (ebook)

Cover layout, illustrations and design by Oscar Fa
Interior formatting by Sophie White

Printed by Kindle Direct Publishing

JO-JO
the Kind Sloth

A children's book about developing self-compassion

Dr Olivia Ong

Joseph Lee

When Jo-Jo came home from school, Mama Sloth came out of her office and saw the sadness in his face.

"I don't think I'm very smart, Mummy," Jo-Jo said.

He burst into tears.

Jo-Jo wiped his eyes and sighed.
"It was the spelling test.
I didn't do as well as my friends."

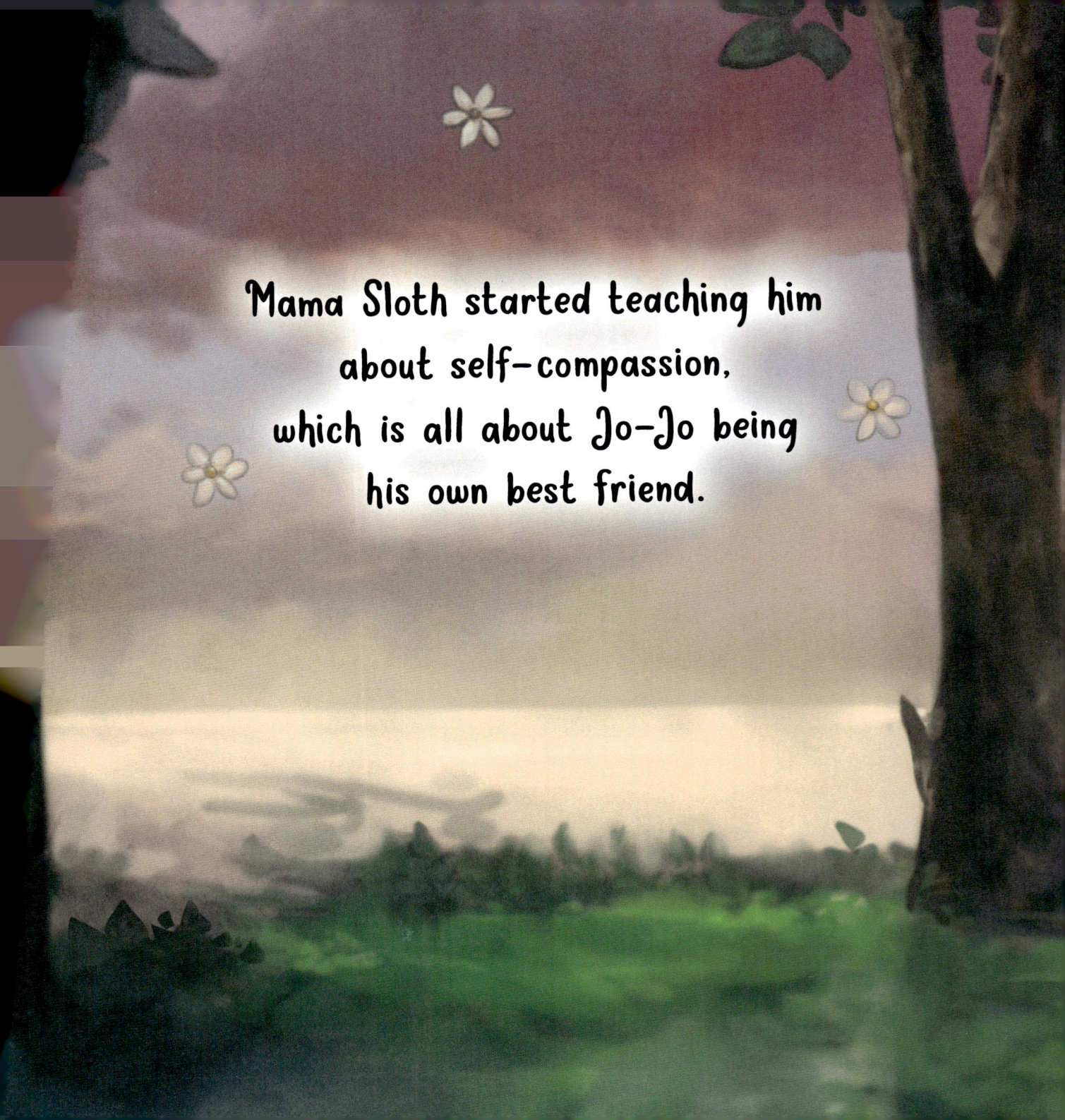

Mama Sloth started teaching him about self-compassion, which is all about Jo-Jo being his own best friend.

Mama Sloth asked Jo-Jo,
"If the same thing happened to your
best friend Tommy, what would you say to him?"

Jo-Jo replied,
"I would try to cheer Tommy up
and tell him to try harder next time.
That it's okay not to do
as well as you'd hoped."

Mama Sloth asked Jo-Jo,
"So, now, you did not do well on your test,
what will you say to yourself?"

Jo-Jo looked at Mama Sloth,
his eyes lit up with excitement, and said,
"I will tell myself that it's okay
and to try harder next time."

"That's right, Jo-Jo," Mama Sloth said.

"This is self-compassion.
It's about being kind to yourself,
about being your own best friend."
She hugged Jo-Jo tight.

Jo-Jo smiled, wide and bright. "Yes, Mummy, I will always be my own best friend, no matter what."

Made in the USA
Las Vegas, NV
30 November 2024